ABBREVIATED LAYS

ABBREVIATED LAYS

Stories of Ancient Rome,
from Aeneas to Pope Gregory I,
in Double-Dactylic Rhyme

Poems by A. T. Reyes

Notes by S. S. O. Edgar

Drawings by C. Herrmann

Oxbow Books

Published by
Oxbow Books, Park End Place, Oxford OX1 1HN

© Poems: Andres T. Reyes; Notes: Swift S. O. Edgar; Drawings:
Christian Herrmann, 2003

ISBN 1 84217 111 9

A CIP record for this book is available from the British Library

This book is available direct from
Oxbow Books, Park End Place, Oxford OX1 1HN
(Phone: 44-(0)1865-241249; Fax: 44-(0)1865-794449)

and

The David Brown Book Company
PO Box 511, Oakville, CT 06779, USA
(Phone: 860-945-9329; Fax: 860-945-9468)

or from the website

www.oxbowbooks.com

Printed in Great Britain at
Maney Publishing
Leeds

CONTENTS

PREFACE

In the pantheon of poetic forms, the double-dactyl must rank among the lesser orders. Born in 1951, it is of comparatively recent origin, lacking the punch of the limerick or the pedigree of nonsense verse. Nor was the double-dactyl ever intended for the serious or high-minded, as the poet Anthony Hecht intimates when he describes in *Jiggery-Pokery*, that classic compendium of double-dactyl poetry, the moment of its conception at a lunch shared by Hecht, the Classics Professor Paul Pascal, and Pascal's wife Naomi in the American Academy at Rome:

> It must have been half way through the saltimbocca that Paul and I became alive to the enormous possibilities latent in Naomi's gentle suggestion. So moved were we that we turned instantly, as if governed by a single impulse, to the Frascati. While it is true that nothing memorable was said, it should be remembered that Bell's famous exclamation was only a response to his own silly clumsiness. Ours was a dignified and pregnant silence, much like Alexander Fleming's when gazing at his mouldy pots. Such moments are hard to describe.
>
> By the end of the afternoon, we had hammered out the nature and details of the form.

Despite the obscurity of its birth, however, the double-dactyl has enjoyed a certain vogue, produced by practitioners as varied as W. H. Auden, Wendy Cope, John Hollander, James Merrill, James Michie, and George Starbuck, aside from Hecht himself.

In part, its persistence at the poetic banquet, like the off-putting presence of a poor relative at a fancy wedding, must be due to its strictness and simplicity. Unlike the clerihew, its British counterpart, the double-dactyl is metrically exact, and the rules governing its substance are formal. To wit (and here we quote Hecht once more):

> The form itself, as it was determined that November day in Rome, is composed of two quatrains of which the last line of the first rhymes with the last line of the second. All the lines except the rhyming ones, which are truncated, are composed of two dactylic feet. The first line of the poem must be a double dactylic nonsense line, like "Higgledy-Piggledy," or "Pocketa-pocketa" (this last, of course, borrowed from *The Secret Life of Walter Mitty*). The second line must be a double dactylic name. And then, somewhere in the poem, though preferably in the second stanza, and ideally in the antepenultimate line, there must be at least one double dactylic line which is *one word long*. (Foreign languages may be employed, and indeed there is a hope that this form

> will restore macaronic verse to the dignity it has not enjoyed since the
> Late Middle Age.)

Such are the bare bones of the double-dactyl. Hecht elaborated further by
pointing out that titles and epithets may be admissible as part of the double-
dactyl names, and that hyphenated forms are to be viewed with suspicion
and acceptable only *in extremis* (*e.g.*, when one needs to get rid of a poem
by three in the morning, before teaching at eight o'clock), if they are to be
accepted at all.

It will be apparent from the above that poems in this volume are more
properly described as in double-dactylic rhyme, rather than as double-
dactyls *per se*. It has been beyond whatever ingenuity the authors possess to
ensure that all second lines are restricted to nomenclature alone. On occasion, a verb or participle or some other happily helpful set of syllables has
been called in, like a volunteer-fireman, for assistance. While real poets will
no doubt frown at this practice of allowing verbal riffraff into the exclusive
confines of the Second-Line-of-the-Double-Dactyl Club, it has seemed
better, in the interests of mental equilibrium and the maintenance of a
more-or-less sunny disposition, to assume a looser, less rigid stance.

Secondly, with one exception, instead of double-dactyl nonsense syllables
in the first line, Latin tags and expressions have been substituted.
"Higgledy-Piggledy", "Pocketa-pocketa", "Jiggery-Pokery", and the like
are fine phrases, but the patience of even the most accommodating reader
would surely be tried by the constant repetition of these when attached to
what is, at its best, the work of a poetaster. Since, these days, Latin words
and tags are considered nonsense anyway by a majority of the population, it
has seemed no bad thing to use, as the first line, a variety of these that are
in double-dactylic rhythm, especially when their sense is somehow apposite
to a particular poem. Some fortuitously meet the criterion that nonsense
phrases have repeating sounds (*e.g.*, *manibus pedibus, nomine Domini, toties
quoties*), but other tags have no special iterative quality. All Latin, including
any found in this introduction, is translated in an index at the end of the
volume.

For the most part also, syllables with -iu- or -ia- are to be read as two
syllables (*e.g.*, "Ju-li-us", rather than "Jul-ius"). Occasionally, however, the
English for certain names and common nouns requires the use of just one
syllable. This inconsistency of pronunciation too will not, we hope, detract
from the reader's enjoyment.

The composition of the poems themselves began as a result of the conca-
tenation of three events in early March 2001: a chance conversation with a
Sixth-Form girl (Katherine Collier) about the poetry of Anthony Hecht;
the recent completion in a third-year Latin class of a reading of Cicero's

first speech on the Catilinarian conspiracy; and the experience over Easter of a tedium and heat so great during survey-work atop a mountain near Petra that, as one of the authors was grasping the end of a measuring tape, his wits wandered sufficiently from the matter at hand to realise that "Catilinarian" was diplodactylic. On that hot day in Jordan, after the studious contemplation of rather a lot of broken cornices and capitals, this seemed an interesting and even awesome thought, not on the level of those attributed to Cortez on Darien, to be sure, but striking nonetheless. Shortly thereafter, a small poem on Cicero was born, surreptitiously inscribed on the inside of a discarded box of slide-film.

And that, on the face of it, would have been that. But in the same way that eating peanut after peanut becomes an obsession, double-dactyl words continued to present themselves bidden or unbidden, and eventually a second poem on Romulus and Remus manifested itself. It then seemed somehow necessary to bridge the chronological gap between Romulus and Cicero. Unfortunately, the next double-dactyls were the ones on Caligula, Nero, and Aeneas. But after four months, the survey having ended and a spring-term at School having passed, a reasonable double-dactyl history of Rome emerged, like a slightly embarrassed phoenix, from these clandestine poetic ashes.

During that spring-term, some of the poems appeared (carefully couched as "anonymous" and "of unknown or untraceable origin") as part of "extra-credit" questions on the tests, quizzes, and examinations of the second-year Latin classes, to establish whether or not the sense of a poem was at all comprehensible, let alone amusing. After several awkward silences from pupils and much revision, the text came into the hands of an interested Fourth-Form party who provided the historical notes, preparing a first draft in the summer of 2001. Yet further revision has resulted in the present text. In the spring of 2002, another boy, then in the Fourth Form, offered to draw cartoon-illustrations.

We are all grateful to the different second-year Latin classes for having endured so much by way of double-dactylic rhyme. It is hoped, nevertheless, that these poems — rudimentary mnemonic devices at their most serious, pleasant diversions at their best — will at least have lightened and leavened the school-day. For criticisms, corrections, help, and improvements, we also thank Josh Adams, Ann Alexander, Bunny Bispham, Katherine Bradley, Vernon Cassin, Katherine Collier, Ann Emerson, John Finley, Richard Fox, Byron Fuller, Victoria Harnish, Ned Henry, Carl Herrmann, Pooky Herrmann, Robert Humphreville, Liz Laws, Anna Lethbridge, Nancy Lynn, Judith McKenzie, Martina Minas-Nerpal, Julian Petri, David Ross, Hugh Sackett, Rogers Scudder, Allison Siegenthaler, Jennifer Stager, the Sulkowski family, Paul Windels, and especially John

DeStefano, whose eagle-eye, acute ear, and extensive notes have assisted this enterprise enormously. To Liz Rosindale and Anna Thrush of Maney Publishing and David Brown of Oxbow Books are owed thanks for the production and publication of this volume. We are grateful too to Groton School and the trustees of the Dillon Fund for every kindness and to the Headmaster, William Polk, who has supported this project from its inception. For her help and her cuisine, we must mention also Mme Micheline Myers. The next paragraph notwithstanding, this book stands as testament to her teaching and inspiration.

Our greatest debt is to Mr Warren Myers to whom this volume is dedicated on the occasion of his retirement from Groton School as Classics Master after thirty-two years. Both the writing of this volume and the raising of the printing subvention have resulted from the collaborative efforts of his former pupils as a way of showing their gratitude to that schoolmaster who, more than any other, has shown what it means to be human.

> Quondam discipuli
> Hoc dant Myersio
> ("Semper lasciva mens
> Gaudium est.").
>
> Gratias agimus,
> Sapientissime
> Magister optime:
> "Frigidus es!"

The above may be translated loosely — very loosely — as follows: "The former pupils of Warren Myers dedicate this book to him (who once memorably remarked while reading Catullus' poetry 'A dirty mind is a joy forever') as a way of thanking him for his wisdom, erudition, and excellent teaching over the years; to lapse into vernacular, and to use his own translation of local school argot: 'You are so cool!'."

A. T. R.
S. S. O. E.
C. H.

Groton, Massachusetts
Easter Sunday 2003

INVOCATION

Musa Pieria,
Clio, Calliope,
Sing of the civili-
Sation of Rome:

Sing of Troy's Fall, Caesar's
Invincibility;
Sing as you will — only
Fill in this tome!

Clio and Calliope (muses of legend)
Two of a large family of nine, Clio and Calliope were the muses of history and
epic, respectively.

Forsan et haec olim,
Pius Aeneas wept:
"I get no kick from Cam-
Panian songs.

Alcohol renders me
Unnecessarily
Tearful, since my heart to
Dido belongs."

Aeneas (legendary hero of the Trojan War)

This mythical man is credited with having founded the Italian settlement whose people would migrate to the land that several hundred years later would become the site of Rome. Aeneas had fled from Troy in Asia Minor and sailed to Carthage in Africa where he met Queen Dido with whom he consorted, initially and presumably uncomfortably, in a cave during a thunder-storm. But he then abandoned his girlfriend, using the excuse — a novel one for the time — that he had to go found a new kingdom in Italy, as prescribed by Fate.

3

Quoad mobilia,
Youthful Ascanius
Ordered a move from his
Latian home:

"Cities make better sites
Archaeological.
Let's move to what will be
Roma, sweet Rome."

Ascanius (legendary figure of the Trojan War)

Ascanius was the product of Aeneas and his first wife Creusa. Like most teen-aged children, he disliked, for no apparent reason, Daddy's way of doing things, and so he moved his father's Italian settlement to Alba Longa, which would later develop into Rome.

Proprio nomine,
Remus to Romulus:
"Had I been favoured, named
Founder supreme,

Winning the augury
Ornithological,
I would be worshipped, and
Rome would be Reme."

Romulus and Remus (eighth century BC)

Sons of the war-god Mars and nursed by a wolf, these twin brothers decided to found a city in 753 BC. Each wanted to name the city after himself; so to settle the argument, they went to separate hills. Over Romulus' head flew twelve vultures, but over Remus' head flew only six. It was therefore clear that the city should bear the name of Romulus. A poor loser, Remus complained and was killed by his brother. By dint of this act, considered incredibly macho in the eighth century, Romulus became History's only he-man suckled by a she-wolf.

Praedium rusticum,
Spouse of a Sabine girl,
Doing the dishes, then
Building a shelf,

Yearned still for warfare: "How
Stereotypical!
Capturing, I am now
Captive myself."

The Rape of the Sabine Women (eighth century BC)

The Sabines were a people living near Rome in its early years of existence. When the Romans grew tired of their own women (who were no doubt relieved), once they had realised there were not enough to go around, they invited the Sabines to their local games. There, they abducted the Sabine women, who became the progenetrices of Rome.

Astra per aspera,
Romulus, king of the   sky.
Quirinal, older and,
Hating to die,   the

Chanced an experience of   to
Paranormality.
Caught in   flew
          a
            w   he
              h
      d,   i
      n   r
      i   l
        w

The Disappearance of Romulus (eighth century BC)

It is said that Romulus did not die, but instead vanished to the heavens where he was deified, becoming Quirinus, god of "organised social totality", a task for which his earlier training as Roman overlord prepared him well.

Sic transit gloria,
Tarquin *Superbus* re-
Gretted his son craved the
Opposite sex:

"He's at that stage of his
Endocrinology.
Hormones are rampant; so
I am not *rex*."

The Tarquin family (sixth century BC)

There were two Roman kings from this family: Tarquin the Elder (*Priscus*) and Tarquin the Proud (*Superbus*). The second of these produced a son, Sextus (which literally means "sixth" in Latin), who raped a woman named Lucretia. This appalling assertion of male dominance and the resultant bad publicity forced Tarquin *Superbus* to abdicate, but he tried to retake the throne later, only to be foiled by …

Vivat res publica,
Lucius Junius
Brutus was teased at his
School and felt hurt.

Tears were succeeded by
Irascibility:
"I kissed my Mum — should I
Rather kiss dirt?"

... Lucius Junius Brutus (late sixth century BC)

Not the Brutus who killed Julius Caesar, this one was a cousin of the Tarquins who became consul in 509 BC. It had been prophesied to him and his relations that whoever kissed his mother first would be the new leader of Rome after the expulsion of the kings. Brutus, a proto-environmentalist, understood immediately that since the earth was the mother of all, he had better eat dirt as quickly as possible, and so he did.

Suo periculo,
Mucius Scaevola
Lost his right hand and com-
Pounded his woes.

Lacking a talent for
Ambidexterity,
He was in need of op-
Posable toes.

Mucius *Scaevola* (late sixth century BC)

When King Lars Porsenna of the nearby Etruscans attacked Rome to help restore the Tarquins, a Roman soldier named Mucius infiltrated the enemy camp, but was captured. Having been told that the punishment would be the loss of his right hand if he did not tell Lars something frightfully useful, Mucius had the presence of mind to realise that the gods had given him two hands for a reason. He placed his right hand in a fire conveniently nearby and burnt it off. Porsenna then surrendered, reasoning that, if he had to fight an army of men as brave as Mucius (and as pleased to play with fire as pyromaniacs at a barbecue), he would surely lose. After this affair, Mucius was given the Latin nickname "*Scaevola*", meaning "left-handed".

Nomina omina,
Cocles Horatius
Swam in full armour: "I'm
Pop-eyed, assailed,

Ormolu-armoured, with
Corporeality —
Why do I feel this a
Comic-strip tale?"

Horatius *Cocles* (late sixth century BC)

During another Etruscan attack, Roman soldiers proved Lars Porsenna's notions regarding their bravery wrong, when they fled into Rome and left three men to defend the only bridge across the Tiber river which passed alongside the city. One of these, Horatius, fended off the enemy, while the others destroyed the bridge. He then jumped into the Tiber, as the enemy glowered on the other side, feeling themselves, unlike Horatius, too encumbered by battle-gear to make the swim. Horatius suffered only one injury, the loss of an eye, for which the Romans awarded him a nickname (their apparent equivalent of the Purple Heart): "*Cocles*", meaning "one-eyed".

A DOUBLE-DACTYL REBUS

```
        a    n   s
6th  T   r  u  iu
        q  i
m  +  Saa,
Rome
"Give  U  Gii!


        S

I'm              no
          s,
syllables  x  12;

N    E,
   E
M   i
¡POW!i!"
```

REBUS TRANSLATION

(Higgledy-piggledy)
Sextus Tarquinius
M(arches on) Rome and says,
"Give (up,) you guys!

I'm s(peaking) s(lowly), no
Dodecasyllables;
Anyone (crosses) me,
POW! (in) the eyes!"

The Death of Sextus Tarquinius (died *circa* 499 or 496 BC)
Sextus Tarquinius escaped Rome after Lucretia's rape and accompanied his father
and Lars Porsenna in their legendary fight to gain the city. A failure and loser to
the end, he died in the attempt.

Malum prohibitum,
Appius Claudius
Liked a large weapon (a
Magnum, he'd say),

Whispering, "Argument's
Inefficacious.
Go ahead, pleb; won't you
Please make my day?"

Appius Claudius (late sixth–early fifth centuries BC)

A Sabine who strove for peace with the Romans, Claudius went to Rome when war broke out between the two peoples in 504 BC. Because of his efforts, he was accepted into the patrician class, but like other political or social converts, he was prone to a certain over-zealousness. In 495 BC, elected consul, he tried to eradicate poverty by the radical, if effective, policy of killing poor people, forcing the plebeians to withdraw to the Mons Sacer, a hill three miles outside of Rome.

Supra memoriam,
Coriolanus at-
Tacked Rome from exile, 'til
Mummy said, "Why,

You're not derived from my
Deoxyribonu-
Cleotides: stop that (and
Now eat some pie)!"

Gnaeus Marcius Coriolanus (early fifth century BC)

The Romans expelled Coriolanus from Rome because he opposed the redistri-
bution of grain to help feed the plebeians, who, he felt, were already too seedy. In
exile, he became the leader of the Volscians, a barbaric tribe to the north, and
waged a successful war against Rome, reaching the city-walls. There his mother
and wife told him off, and he, a curiously hen-pecked historical figure, ended his
campaign.

Summa res publica,
Called, Cincinnatus left
Tilling to fend off the
Aequian crowd.

Modestly, not like some
Megalomaniacs
(*E.g.*, in *Bridge over*
Kwaî), he then ploughed.

Lucius Quinctius Cincinnatus (mid-fifth century BC)

Former consul Cincinnatus was called to serve as military dictator when the tribe of the Aequi threatened Rome in 458 BC. A gentleman-farmer who fortunately knew how to wield more than just ploughs and threshing-equipment, he assembled an army and carried out his charge in a fortnight, after which he returned to his modest farm, turning down all rewards and power offered to him.

Bis dat qui cito dat,
Soldiers of Manlius
Fought off the Gauls and then
Went off to see

Girlfriends, who thought their pride
Incomprehensible:
"No more damned geese", one cried.
"Come on; goose me!"

Marcus Manlius Capitolinus (early fourth century BC)

In 390 BC, the Gauls attacked Rome from two sides. The Romans did not know about the second front until the geese on the Capitoline hill, seeing the Gauls and fearing for their livers, made such an uproar that Manlius and his soldiers realised something (in this case, someone) was up. They reached the scene just as the Gauls were about to sack the government buildings, right on time to claim another Roman victory.

Tempus in ultimum,
General Regulus
Would not concede Cartha-
Ginian terms.

"I can stand torture and
Trinitrotoluene,
Toenail extractions and
Flesh-eating worms."

Marcus Atilius Regulus (mid-third century BC)

Clearly not a man easily given to letting his hair down and knocking back a few drinks with his pals (if he had any) at the local tavern, this Roman general was successful on several occasions during the First Punic War between Rome and Carthage. At Tunis, most notably, he refused to water down his harsh peace terms. The war dragged on, and when Regulus was captured, he refused to be part of a prisoner exchange that would have allowed his freedom. He thus died a prisoner.

Vindex iniuriae,
Hannibal, nine years old,
Urged by King Hamilcar,
Managed to say,

"Even if I become
Octogenarian,
Romans I still shall hate —
Now can I play?"

Hannibal (247–183/2 BC)

This ingenious Carthaginian general, legend had it, was asked by his father to swear eternal enmity to the Romans as a child. Hannibal acceded to his father's request, nursing throughout his early youth much the same feelings toward Rome that the Spanish Inquisition would have toward heresy.

Alteri sic tibi,
Hannibal's elephant
Back from his travels — and
This wasn't nice —

Brought his friends nothing: no
Memorabilia,
T-shirt, or *filia*
(Cheap at the price).

The Second Punic War (218–202 BC)

Thinking that travel through southern Italy could be rather uncivilised, Hannibal decided to attack Rome from the north. In order to get to northern Italy, he crossed the Alps, a feat then thought impossible. In the early stages of the war in Italy, Hannibal routed the Roman army with his brilliant tactics and his elephants, creatures foreign to the local countryside. But once the Roman generals had recovered from the shock of a northern attack and the sight of animals duller than third-declension nouns, the reader will not be surprised to learn that they came back to defeat Hannibal.

Pondere numero,
Fabius Maximus,
Asked by the Senators
How to proceed

Fighting such creatures of
Ponderability,
Answered quite drily, "With
Caution indeed."

Quintus Fabius Maximus (mid-third century BC)

The first Roman general to have consistent success against Hannibal, Fabius won his battles by avoiding fights with the Carthaginian army. This unorthodox and counterintuitive means of conducting a war confused the Carthaginians, who were not therefore at peak performance when Fabius actually decided to attack. This strategy, now called "Fabian Tactics", earned him the nickname "*Cunctator*" or "Delayer."

Socius criminis,
Publius Scipio
Published an ad for a
Friendship long-term:

"I am desirable, like
Africocentrism;
Animal-lover — but
No pachyderms."

Publius Scipio Africanus (236–183 BC)

Scipio was the Roman general most instrumental in putting an end to the Second Punic War. He gave Hannibal his final loss at the Battle of Zama in Africa, and the Romans, as ever open to a good naming-opportunity, called him "*Africanus*" or "the African."

IF HANNIBAL HAD BECOME
HARD-OF-HEARING
AFTER ALL THAT FIGHTING

Maximum animal,
General Hannibal,
Hurled
    down
        to
            Hades, asked,
"That dog is who?"

"CERBERUS." "Serpico?
Serbo-Croatian?
Snoopy?" "NO, CER–BE–RUUUUS!"
"Spot? Scooby-Doo?"

The Death of Hannibal (183 or 182 BC)

After having been handed several losses by the Roman troops, Hannibal fled to Bithynia to escape surrendering himself to enemy forces. The Romans sent an envoy to kill him and end the threat his existence posed to the state, but in order to preempt assassination, Hannibal committed suicide by drinking poison. There is no historical evidence to suggest that Hannibal was hard of hearing, but there is also none to suggest his ears were in tip-top shape.

Hahahae! Hahahee!
Plautus to Terence: "We
Need something fresh, with no
Love-sick twins — well?

"How about shows with tough
Sociopolitics,
Hard-hitting grittiness?"
"They'll never sell."

Titus Maccius Plautus (active *circa* 205–184 BC) and Publius Terentius Afer (active in the 160s BC)

Not just gag-writers, but also the leading humorists of their respective times, Plautus and Terence borrowed (some say stole) from the plots of their Greek forebears and developed the formulae that have allowed the comedies of Shakespeare and Molière to thrive for the highbrow and the films of the Marx Brothers and the Three Stooges to proliferate for the lowbrow.

Ultima ratio,
Cato the Elderly,
Though in old age, would not
Give it a rest,

Ever sententious, a
Proto-Polonius,
Muttering, "*Carthago*
Delenda est."

Marcus Porcius Cato the Elder (234–149 BC)

After twenty-six years in the Roman army, Cato was appointed Censor. Rather than walk about counting people, however, he used this office to condemn noble over-indulgences. When the nobles understandably tired of this, they sent him off to Carthage as a diplomat. But seeing that the city was flourishing, Cato, the most undiplomatic of men, decided its very existence threatened Rome's power, and at the end of every speech in the Senate, he would solemnly and tiresomely commend Carthage's complete destruction. He was thus a major proponent of the Third Punic War (149–146 BC).

Rebus sic stantibus,
Gaius Sempronius
Gracchus, as tribune, en–
Countered some fuss

When his designs were deemed
Unconstitutional:
"Last time that I do what
My brother does!"

The Gracchi Brothers (mid–second century BC)

Although patricians, Tiberius and Gaius Gracchus believed that plebeians deserved more rights than they had and perhaps even a respectable amount of land. As tribunes, the brothers fought for the lower classes and won several concessions for them. But regrettably, the Gracchi themselves possessed more brains than sense. When the conservatives ceased to concede, it was conceived that the brothers's actions were illegal. Both were killed, Tiberius, the elder, in 133 BC, and Gaius, ten years later.

Non licet omnibus,
Sulla Cornelius
Thought that the plebs were too
Much on the make.

Raging, he acted with
Irritability:
"Get me a knife! I could
Murder! A stake!"

Lucius Cornelius Sulla (*circa* 138–79 BC)

Initially working under his future enemy Gaius Marius, Sulla used bribery to climb the social ladder, and, the very model of a modern military dictator, he took over Rome, executing his former allies. A rabid conservative, Sulla was indefatigable, but unsubtle, in his attempts to maintain the privileges of aristocracy: his methods entailed the loss of his opponents' heads.

Morte miserrima,
Rock of Tarpeia, the
Punishment whence Romans

l

    e

      a

      p

      t

      to

      th–

      eir

    d o o m:

Sulla tossed all of the
Tergiversational,
Criminal traitors, and
Now there's no room.

The Tarpeian Rock

This rock on the Capitoline hill was named after Tarpeia, an eighth century BC version of Benedict Arnold (but better-looking), who fancied the jewellery worn on the left arms of some Sabine marauders. She struck a deal for these trinkets and agreed to let them into one of the temples. But after entering, the men showed their gratitude to Tarpeia by taking a broad view of the word "jewellery" and smothering her with their shields, also worn on their left arms. From that time, murderers and traitors were thrown to their deaths from the spot where these events allegedly took place.

THE SHORTEST GLADIATOR-MATCH EVER

Gladium stringere,
"Rebel-slave Spartacus,
Stands in that corner; here,
Italy's Pride!

Both come out fighting with
Gladiatorial
Jabbing … some stabbing … oops!
Italy's … died."

The Revolt of Spartacus (73–71 BC)

Spartacus was one of many slaves-turned-gladiators, but he is distinguished from the others by the relative success of his rebellion against oppression. He was resourceful, brave, strong, and intelligent, but there is as yet no evidence that in physical appearance he matched the cinematic qualities of Kirk Douglas.

MEMO TO THE ROMAN NAVY

Maria omnia
Pompey the Great to the
Naval fleet: 6 *a.m.* —
Set out for sea.

12 *p.m.* — Terminate
Mediterranean
Pirate-ships. 4 *p.m.* —
Head home for tea.

Gnaeus Pompeius Magnus (106 BC–48 BC)
A political rival of Julius Caesar, Pompey was a great general who, having been
ordered by the Senate in 67 BC to rid the Mediterranean of pirates within the year,
carried out his task in three months. He was perhaps tempting fate by calling himself *Magnus* (the Great) from 81 BC, but he never lost a battle until he was defeated
by his more ingenious rival.

Mores et tempora,
Tullius Cicero
Versified, "Best for Rome?
My consulate!"

Sniffed a conspirator
Catilinarian,
"Please, no more poetry;
Simply orate!"

Marcus Tullius Cicero (106–43 BC)

Cicero was a great orator, a fair philosopher, and a terrible poet, a fact of which his contemporaries made him well aware. Consul in 63 BC, he thwarted Catiline's conspiracy to kill him and overthrow the government. Cicero celebrated by executing several of the conspirators, publishing four excellent speeches on the subject, and composing more bad poetry.

Inops consilii,
Publius Clodius
Wore ladies' outfits that
Earned him some stares.

Still, as a businessman
Entrepreneurial,
With the right clothes, he could
Manage affairs.

Publius Clodius *Pulcher* (*circa* 92–52 BC)

Clodius desperately wanted to see the *Bona Dea* festival to which only women were admitted, but as this was before the days of the miracles of modern science, he did the next best thing and cross-dressed. Cicero proved him guilty of violating that ceremony's sanctity, but Clodius bribed the judges and gained an acquittal, becoming a bitter enemy of the orator in the process. In 52 BC, Clodius, by then an aging glamour-boy, died in a most unglamourous fashion. He was attacked and killed by a mob.

Multis cum lacrimis,
Gaius Valerius,
Known as Catullus, wrote:
"Lesbia, my dream,

Live with me, love with me
Heterosexually,
Day in and day out and
With lots of cream."

Gaius Valerius Catullus (*circa* 84–54 BC)

A significant selection of Catullus' work comprises poems of light rhythm, extolling his love for a woman pseudonymously known as Lesbia, unfortunately already married. But neither Catullus nor the lady in question found that inconvenient fact detrimental to their frequent and inventive amatory tumbling.

Nihil ex nihilo,
Titus Lucretius
Grasped that his theories
Made no great gains:

"Atoms are ultimate
Fundamentalities;
Split them in half — and then
Nothing remains."

Titus Lucretius Carus (*circa* 94–55 or 51 BC)
Lucretius was a great philosopher whose most famous work was the long poem
De Rerum Natura (*On the Nature of Things*) in six books. The second book dealt
with atoms and also developed in rudimentary form the theory of a multi-verse,
long before that became a fashionable topic among physicists and writers of
science-fiction.

Casus fortuitus,
General Julius
Fumed at the Sibyl's res–
Ponse, "Is that all?

Years of campaigning, yet
Reputability,
Simply because of a
Theme-park in Gaul?"

The Gallic Wars (58–51 BC)

The unprecedented movement of peoples from Helvetia (Switzerland) into Gaul encouraged that best-known of all Romans, Julius Caesar, then a political general intent on out-manoeuvering his rivals, to lead an army across the Alps to protect Roman interests. In Gaul, he consolidated his power-base within the military, quite apart from extending Roman territory and influence, while establishing the basis for the adventures of Asterix and Obelix.

Alea iacta est,
Julius Caesar, once
At a casino, com-
Plained, "I've not lost!

Pace those claiming odd
Irregularities,
Nothing was loaded when
My dice were tossed!"

Gaius Julius Caesar (102–44 BC)

Returning from Gaul with the intention of waging war against his political rivals, Julius Caesar crossed the Rubicon river into Italy and exclaimed, "*Alea iacta est* (The die is cast.)." The gamble was successful, and Caesar hit the proverbial jack-pot. He became dictator for life in 48 BC, a position he had expected to hold for appreciably longer than the next four years.

Tempus me deficit,
Consular Julius,
Keenly aware that there
Had to be done Th-

Ousands of tasks said, "As
Generalissimo,
I need more time — so I'll
Add a new month."

The Introduction of the Julian Calendar (45 BC)

The most lasting of Julius Caesar's many reforms in Rome was his adoption in 45 BC of a new calendar-system with a year made up of 365 days and twelve months, one of which would be named for him. The previous year, 46 BC, had had 445 days in it — far too long, by any reckoning, although, as with any good facial cream, it did have the advantage of slowing down the aging process.

Malevolentia,
Brutus and Cassius
Checked in their books for a
Mutual date.

"Kalends seems busy." "Nones?"
"Physiotherapy."
"Later then." "March?" "Is the
Ides much too late?"

Marcus Junius Brutus (85–42 BC) and Gaius Cassius Longinus (died 42 BC)

In 44 BC, Julius Caesar had gained so much power that it frightened the Senate. Brutus and Cassius, who were numbered among Caesar's friends, decided to assassinate him on the Ides of March (the fifteenth of that month). Caesar's wife, as well as a sooth-sayer and several omens, had told Caesar to beware of this day, so legend has it, but the gods could only do so much by way of warning. As Caesar was stabbed, he gasped his last words, "καὶ σύ, τέκνον (Even you, my child)," but it was all Greek to the Senate, who killed him anyway.

Probum non poenitet,
Marcus Antonius,
Subject to prurient
Interests and jeers,

Nonetheless wanted life
Egyptological:
"Friends, Romans, countrymen,
End me your leers!"

Marcus Antonius (*circa* 84–30 BC)

After a successful military career, Marcus Antonius (or Mark Antony, as he is better known) earned political office as a result of his friend Julius Caesar's influence, eventually sharing the consulship with him in 44 BC. After a couple of defeats at the hands of his rival Octavian (later Caesar Augustus), Antony abandoned Rome and departed for Egypt, encouraged in this decision by a desire to consort with the lovely Queen Cleopatra, whom age could not wither, and whose infinite variety custom could not stale.

Acta est fabula,
Actium Admirals
Claimed, "The Egyptians went
Full steam ahead,

Tactics as airy as
Phantasmagoria;
We called a *spado* a
Spado instead."

The Battle of Actium (31 BC)

At this naval battle, Caesar's adopted son Octavian defeated the combined forces of Cleopatra and Mark Antony, thereby consolidating his hold over the Roman Empire. Immediately after the defeat at Actium, just off the western coast of Greece, Cleopatra fled back to Egypt and committed suicide by applying to her breast an adder (a type of snake, not the more deadly reptile commonly called an accountant).

Ars amatoria,
Caesar Augustus in-
Structed Maecenas: "Love
Lyrics obscene

Speed up my heart and make
Cardiovascular
Exercise necessary;
Please keep them clean."

Caesar Augustus (63 BC–AD 14; ruled 31 BC–AD 14)

Octavian later became known as Caesar Augustus. In the years following Julius Caesar's death, he consolidated the lands of North Africa, the Middle East, Sicily, and Europe. A patron of the arts in conjunction with the wealthy playboy Maecenas, Augustus promoted the writing of poetry that encouraged a certain morality, though neither he nor Maecenas could claim that his own circle was without blemish. These days, Augustus is probably best known for the annual mention of his name during Christmas pageants, since the Gospel-writers say he decreed the census of the Roman world that led Mary and Joseph to initiate birthing procedures in the little town of Bethlehem.

Architectonicus,
Builder Vitruvius,
Engineer, author, ex–
Claimed, "It's a cinch:

Temple-height equals twice
Intercolumnial
Distance times four-fifths pi,
Plus half an inch ...★

★*i.e.,* height $= (4/5)\pi\ [2(\text{intercolumniation})] + 1/2"$. Is that clear? There will be a quiz tomorrow."

Vitruvius Pol(l)io (*circa* first century BC)

Vitruvius' fame rests on his treatise *De Architectura* (*On Architecture*), a guide to ancient engineering no less valuable for what it says about Greek and Roman times than its subsequent use as a handbook for builders of the Renaissance. Without Vitruvius, there may well have been no Palladio, Michaelangelo, or da Vinci, and the skylines of perhaps half a dozen major cities would no more recall the Classical orders than the moonscape would resemble an Acapulco beach.

Concupiscentia,
Caesar's girl, Julia
Daily sought pleasure's ex-
Cesses: "More wine!"

"Race at top-speed, as at
Indianapolis!"
"Sin in a temple? It's
Simply divine!"

Julia (39 BC–*circa* AD 14)

If there were ever a girl that "had it all," Julia was certainly that girl. The only daughter of Augustus — and almost certainly a spoilt brat as a result — Julia had power, prestige, intelligence, wealth, sex appeal, beauty, and wit. She married three times (the last time to the Emperor Tiberius), engaged in several adulterous affairs, and (probably) managed to get the poet Ovid exiled in the bargain. Julia's excesses prompted an exasperated Augustus to banish her from Rome in 2 BC, and she died of starvation far from home.

Artes ingenuae,
Quintus Horatius
Felt that the fad for the
Epic was through:

"No Virgil, I prefer
Paraklausithyra,
Odes, satires, epodes, *pro-*
Pemptika too."

Quintus Horatius Flaccus (65–8 BC) and Publius Vergilius Maro (70–19 BC)

Horace and Virgil were among the poets under the patronage of Maecenas and Augustus. Born to a poor father and briefly a military man, Horace wrote, most famously, four books of odes, coining such phrases as "*Carpe diem!*" for eventual use on bumper stickers. Virgil wrote two extended works on farming and the pastoral life, known as the *Georgics* and *Eclogues*. Towards the end of Augustus' reign, he composed the *Aeneid*, an epic of twelve books in the Homeric tradition, which he never finished. Saying that Virgil is the greatest of all Roman poets would be like saying that Romeo was "rather fond" of Juliet.

Tabulae publicae,
Ovid to Livy crowed,
"History's a plagiarist's
Craft, is it not?

Best are *epyllia*
Aetiological,
Not those *Annales*." Said
Livy, "That's rot."

Publius Ovidius Naso (43 BC–AD 17) and Titus Livius Patavinus (59 BC–AD 17)

A prolific writer, Ovid transcribed many common legends into poetry in his work *The Metamorphoses*, which includes the tale of Pyramus and Thisbe, an episode parodied in Shakespeare's *A Midsummer Night's Dream*. He also combined successfully high-mindedness with gutter-mentality by writing an instruction manual in elegiac couplets on how to pick up women in Rome. Livy was an antiquarian who wrote a multi-volume history of Rome which must take ultimate blame for such sword-and-sandal sagas as Elizabeth Taylor's *Cleopatra* and Russell Crowe's *Gladiator*.

Gratia gratiam,
Caesar Tiberius
Read the *Enquirer* and
Shouted, "No way!

I detest shops with such
Paraphernalia:
Amazon Hot Com, Sin-
Tendo, She-Bay."

Emperor Tiberius (42 BC–AD 37; ruled AD 14–37)

The second Roman emperor, Tiberius was the adopted son of Augustus and commander of the Roman army until his adoptive father's death. Late in his life, he left Rome, never to return because of his dislike for the city and his quite proper wish to relieve his sexual desires away from the populace, without frightening the horses.

Materfamilias,
Domina Livia
Railed that the post to her
Son, far from Rome,

Came back stamped *Address is*
Unverifiable:
"Emp'ror Tiberius,
E. T., 'phone home!'"

Livia Drusilla (58 BC–AD 29)

Wife of Augustus and a ruthless manipulator rumoured to have engineered the accession of Tiberius to the Principate, Livia received little thanks from her son for her efforts. The body-count on his behalf included at least five pretenders to the throne, to say nothing of suspicions surrounding her role in Augustus' own death. It is not surprising, therefore, that some believe Tiberius, with so formidable a mother, stayed away from Rome chiefly to avoid her.

Toties quoties,
Gaius Caligula
Made his horse Senator.
That did not pay:

"What a peculiar
Idiosyncracy!
When I want 'aye', he will
Always vote 'neigh'."

Emperor Caligula (12 BC–AD 41; ruled AD 37–41)

Caligula started his reign auspiciously, but encountered a grave illness under which he probably lost his mind. He then became eccentric and blood-thirsty, at one point ordering the Roman army to collect shells north of Gaul to symbolise that Rome had conquered the ocean. Such behaviour the Romans tended to find wearisome, and so, exerting themselves for once, they murdered him.

Sancta simplicitas,
Emperor Claudius
Wondered: "Bank-holidays,
Stopping at night,

Week-end delays on grounds
Parliamentarian,
Tea-time, vacations: just
When do Brits fight?"

Emperor Claudius (10 BC–AD 54; ruled AD 41–54)

Claudius succeeded Caligula after the latter's murder. His reign was marked by the choice of some bad wives who forced him to commit tyrannical acts. In AD 43, Claudius annexed parts of Britain. He was poisoned by his last wife, whose son was …

Noli me tangere,
Emperor Nero re-
Buked the Musician's Guild:
"Haven't you learnt?

No one's to rival me
Musicologically.
Playing with lyres, you're
Apt to get burnt."

... Emperor Nero (AD 37–68; ruled AD 54–68)

In AD 64, Rome experienced a great fire that ravaged the city's wood-based buildings. Nero, according to legend, stood by, lazily stroking his lyre, displaying the
apathy that marked his reign. His ambivalence was matched only by his cruelty,
and family-reunions were fraught affairs, resulting in the murders of his wife,
mother, and step-brother.

A DOUBLE-DACTYL ROMAN ALPHABET

*A*becedaria,
"**B**ritish-born Boudicca,
Colchester-chargers come,
Duly despatched!"

"**E**vidence?" "Excellent
Familiarity:
Generals gathered great
Hostilely-hatched

Info." "*Iceni*, I'll
Lead, lest *Londinium-*
Milites madly march
Netherwards, nigh.

Our opportunities?
Polypugnacious
Quarrels, quests, quiddities!
Ready? Reply!"

So she spoke.
   Then they traveled to
       Uerulamium.

Boudicca (died *circa* AD 61)

Boudicca, warrior-princess, led a British revolt against the invading Romans with her tribe, the Iceni, in the vanguard. Despite her best efforts, the rebellion failed, though Boudicca herself, sometimes called Boadicea, achieved later fame as a feminist icon.

Munus aetherium,
Marcus Manilius,
Author, astronomer,
Autodidact,

Versatile word-smith with
Sesquipedalian
Tendencies only sur-
Vives in some taxt — ualy and poet c lly ccorruptt
manuscripts.

Marcus Manilius (*circa* first century AD)

Manilius was a particular interest of the English poet and Latin professor A. E. Housman, but it is difficult to imagine two more different authors. Whereas Housman took landscape and countryside and love as his themes, Manilius kept his head firmly amongst the stars, writing on the skies and heavens in a manner almost totally void of emotion. His principal work is the *Astronomica*, a long and didactic hexameter poem, difficult to interpret not only because of the obscurity of its subject and language, but also because of the corruptness of the relevant manuscripts.

Annus mirabilis,
Otho, Vitellius,
Galba, Vespasian,
Year 69:

How could it be that those
Julio-Claudians
Managed to keep a con-
Tinuous line?

Year 69

Year 69 began in June 68, when Galba, a distinguished patrician, was recognised as emperor by the Senate. Then in January 69, troops in lower Germany decided that Vitellius, their governor, would be emperor. Meanwhile, Otho, who had hoped to become Galba's heir, decided not to waste any time and usurped the throne instead. Otho then went off to fight Vitellius, but lost and committed suicide. The armies in the east subsequently got in on the fun and declared that Vespasian, who had just suppressed a rebellion in Judaea, was emperor. This time, however, the newly proclaimed leader kept his office, not to mention his head, and ruled for ten years.

Simplex munditiis,
Caesar Vespasian,
Feeling uncomfortable,
Salvaged some pride:

"For the enhancement of
Conviviality,
I'll have to build my own
Toilets inside."

Emperor Vespasian (AD 9–79; ruled AD 69–79)

Vespasian's accession began a decade of peace and construction. As a member of the middle class who had risen through the army, Vespasian knew what Rome was like beyond the city's walls, and he used this understanding successfully to quiet much dissent within the empire, whether through diplomacy or military force. More importantly, he brought plumbing to the Capitol, as Millard Fillmore would do at the White House — a clear example of great minds thinking alike.

Rectus in curia,
Titus, as Emperor,
Banished informers, dis-
Missed catamites,

Passed out relief as an
Environmentalist:
Why did he die, saying,
"Sinned once — that bites!"?

Emperor Titus (AD 39–81; ruled AD 79–81)

As an emperor, Titus was, curiously for a Caesar, a well-liked figure. He followed in his father's footsteps by continuing to rebuild Rome. He also took on the task of repairing the damage of Mount Vesuvius to the towns of Pompeii and Herculaneum. Titus' reputation for goodness is such that his dying admission that he committed "one mistake" has been the subject of much speculation. It has been thought that he regretted not having done something about his younger brother Domitian who, perhaps irked by Titus' goody-two-shoes approach to life, bumped him off and usurped power.

FATHER QUINTILIAN

"*Eloquentissimus*
Doctus Quintilian,
What is the longest in
Latin you've seen?"

"I think *honorifi-*
Cabilitudini-
Tatibus." "What could that
Possibly mean?"

Answer: "with honourablenesses" (Shakespeare uses the word in *Love's Labours Lost*.)

"*Gratias agimus*,
Pater Quintilian,
What is the shortest in
Latin you find?

"I think *brevissima*,
Counterintuitive
Though that be." "Have you a
Literal mind?"

Answer: Yes, since *brevissima* means "shortest."

"*Iterum, iterum,*
Master Quintilian
What is the strangest in
Latin you ken?"

"College abounds with the
Intelligentsia,
Scholars, Professors — so
Go bother them!"

Marcus Fabius Quintilianus (*circa* AD 35–90s)
Quintilian was a schoolmaster with a particular interest in the teaching of grammar and rhetoric. His skills were such that his treatises on these subjects were considered authoritative well into the nineteenth century, and Quintilian himself achieved fame and fortune in his time — no mean feat for a teacher of any age.

Sero, sed serio,
Pliny the Elder to
Pliny the Younger, this
Note from Pompeii:

"*Salve!* The lava is
Incontrovertibly
Lavish. I wish you were …."
(Text's burnt away.)

Pliny the Elder (AD 4–79) and Pliny the Younger (AD 61–112)

Pliny the Elder (Gaius Plinius Secundus Maior) was a natural historian-*cum*-scientist who sacrificed his life for his art by trying to get a closer look at the eruption of Mount Vesuvius in AD 79. Pliny the Younger (Gaius Plinius Caecilius Secundus Iunior), the biological nephew and adopted son of the Elder, was a celebrated orator at an early age and also had an interest in Vesuvius, but he preferred to view the volcano at a safer distance.

DOMITIAN A.D. 81

DOMITIAN A.D. 95

Omnia vanitas,
Caesar Domitian
Dreaded the loss of his
Long, flowing locks.

"Why should I suffer faults
Genealogical?
Death to a Roman who
My portrait mocks."

Emperor Domitian (AD 51–96; ruled AD 81–96)

Domitian succeeded his brother Titus in 81. His rule started out well, but after a few military defeats, he became angry and aggressive, no doubt, as modern psychologists would have it, to compensate for a loss of self-esteem compounded by a corresponding loss of hair. He gloried in the defeat of others, and as with so many other Roman emperors, his wife brought about his eventual demise.

De Oratoribus,
Publius (?) Tacitus
Pondered his future: "I
Don't have the knack!

Poet? Philosopher? Both
Impossibilities!
What should I do? I shall
Have to change tack — and compose sardonic
sentences, lapidary in style, solemn in rhythm, pregnant in meaning and in-
sinuation."

Publius (?) Cornelius Tacitus (*circa* AD 56–after 118)

For someone whose name means "the quiet one," Tacitus wrote rather a lot of
words about his chosen subjects. His major (*i.e.*, longest) works are the *Annals*, a
penetrating study of the Julio-Claudian dynasty from the accession of Tiberius, and
the *Histories*, telling of events from roughly AD 69 to 96. His sharp cynicism and
stylish sentences distinguish his books from those of other Roman historians.

Adspice, prospice,
Nerva, when Emperor,
Irked by the Senate, would
Plaintively note

Prophecies, such as, "By
MMXCIV,
Chariots will fly, and all
Women will vote."

Emperor Nerva (*circa* AD 35–98; ruled AD 96–98)

A visionary and far-sighted man, Nerva ruled for two years following Domitian's death. He brought a calm to the state and generously refrained from proscribing or assassinating his detractors. He had good intentions, but lacked drive, and thus he was a good emperor not for what he did (essentially nothing), but for what he did not do (govern by fear and murder).

Verba iactantia,
Pius, Aurelius,
Trajan, and Hadrian
Vowed that they would

Countermand spin-doctored
Verisimilitude;
They were not Emperors
"Super," but "good."

The Five Good Emperors (AD 96–180)

The phrase "Five Good Emperors" is an old schoolboy-term for Nerva and his four successors: Trajan, Hadrian, Antoninus Pius, and Marcus Aurelius, who presided over a period of extended peace and prosperity within the Roman Empire. As with other famous and fabulous groups composed of strong-minded types (*e.g.*, the Beatles, the Beach Boys, or the Rolling Stones), the end-product was a certain harmony, though there were still strong creative differences between the individual figures that often threatened break-up.

Manibus pedibus,
Trajan the Emperor
Moved on the Danube and
German frontier.

Countering hordes showed no
Pussilanimity.
Vinum and *aqua* were
No match for beer.

Emperor Trajan (AD 53–117; ruled AD 98–117)

Trajan succeeded Nerva in AD 98, and in his nineteen years as emperor, he achieved many military victories, annexing much of the Middle East, including Petra and Mesopotamia, but he could not successfully cross the Danube. He also built many roads, held games, and kept the populace content. His reign issued in a long period of stability — a rare treat in the life of the empire.

Nolo contendere,
Emperor Hadrian
Hoped to incorporate,
Had he the time,

Cities and name them all
Antinoöpolis:
"Tourists may criticise;
There'd be no crime."

Emperor Hadrian (AD 76–138; ruled AD 117–138)
Hadrian successfully established peace at the borders of the empire and within
them, waging relatively few wars and enjoying the tranquillity of Rome — though
his friendship with the young Antinoös, after whom he named the Egyptian city
Antinoöpolis, prompted some gossip amongst the glitteratti.

Medio tempore,
T. Antoninus in-
Gested some Swiss cheese, then
Suffered a stroke.

All Romans mourned. He'd ruled
Unostentatiously:
"Why try to fix something
When it's not broke?"

Emperor Antoninus Pius (AD 86–161; ruled AD 138–161)

Antoninus did nothing major, but kept the empire in the same array as Hadrian had left it. His lack of ambition prevented him from doing anything unnecessary (not a bad idea, as it turned out), and he left Marcus Aurelius with few problems to fix.

Cogito, ergo sum,
Marcus Aurelius
Puzzled his critics who
Wanted to know:

"Are you a Platonist,
Aristotelian,
Epicure, Stoic, a
Sage on the go?"

Emperor Marcus Aurelius (AD 121–180; ruled AD 161–180)

This just emperor, sometimes called "the philosopher," is remembered in predo-minantly good light, as his only grossly objectionable act was the persecution of the odd Christian. What he thought is as important as what he did, and his writing on stoicism, known as his *Meditations*, remains with us as a testimony to his ideals.

Medicus, medicus,
Galen of Pergamon
Listed the things that to-
Day he'd get done:

Cure case of eczema
             agoraphobia
             fever
             gout
             lung-disease
Golf
2 drinks
Fun.

Galen of Pergamon (AD 129–? 199/216)

Galen was a true original. A medical pioneer and general practitioner, with the emphasis on *general*, Galen could conduct brain surgery on a given morning, sever a few spinal cords and experiment on drugs in the afternoon, and then write up his observations in the evening. Given so punishing a daily schedule, it is little short of miraculous that he lived as long as he did. But since Galen was also one of the first to understand the importance of "stress management" in life, this is not as surprising as it may seem.

Ceteris paribus,
Emperor Commodus
Wondered why Hercules
Thrilled him to bits:

"Is it the muscles? My
Hellenophilia?
No — it's the way that the
Lion-skin fits."

Emperor Commodus (AD 161–192; ruled AD 180–192)

The son of Marcus Aurelius, Commodus was self-centred and gloried in blood-sport. He publicly fought with wild animals to show off, and then demanded that the people worship him as the god Hercules. A certain wish-fulfillment then took over, and his death was as bizarre as that contrived for any Greek hero. He was poisoned by one of his concubines and then strangled by a popular athlete.

Fructu, non foliis,
Caesar Septimius
Turned to astrology,
Wanting a bride.

"Julia Domna's not
Infelicissima,
Is she? Or is she a
Tyrannicide?"

Emperor Septimius Severus (AD 145–211; ruled AD 193–211)

A North African, Septimius Severus was of obscure birth, but he rose to become Emperor by defeating several rivals. Addicted to astrology, he married his bride Julia Domna, a highly intellectual, accomplished woman and therefore (to the average Roman) of suspect character — only once his local psychic had approved her horoscope.

Res ipsa loquitur,
Caesar Quintillus was
Ruler but briefly, and
Hence poorly known.

Still, he did do some things
Utilitarian.
He's, for example, the
Name in this poem.

Emperor Quintillus (accession in AD 270)

All one needs to know about Quintillus is simply that he was Emperor in August 270. His reign lasted between seventeen and sixty days long, and he never ruled from Rome.

Vitae curriculum,
Snubbed, Diocletian
Listed his names to im-
Press a young gal:

Pontifex Maximus,
Adiabenicus,
Persicus, Felix In-
Victus, et al.

Emperor Diocletian (AD 245–305; ruled AD 284–305)
Diocletian ruled the eastern part of the empire after it had been divided into two. Following the energetic persecution of Christians, he ended his long reign by abdicating, the result of a long-standing desire to retire to the countryside and, in the absence of television, to watch the grain grow.

CONSTANTINE'S COMPLAINT

Nomine Domini,
Emperor Constantine
Saw a psychiatrist,
Nerves all awry.

"Pagan and Christian; from
Constantinopolis,
Rome, too; love East and West —
Schizoid, am I?"

Panis angelicus,
Constantine's therapist
Said: "Contradictions are
Part of the norm.

What makes me worry's hal-
Lucinogenesis:
Visions near bridges and
Sights cruciform."

Emperor Constantine (AD 272 or 273–337; ruled AD 307–337)

Constantine converted to Christianity during a military campaign when he had a vision of the cross in the sky and heard the words, "*In hoc signo, vinces* (By this sign, you will conquer)." Today, seeing such visions and hearing such voices would result in some sort of institutionalisation, but back then, Constantine was not considered abnormal, and he happily went on to encourage Christianity within Rome. He then moved the capital of the empire to Constantinople, now Istanbul.

Domine, salva nos,
Emperor Julian
Cried apostatically
Contra the Pope:

"Pie-eyed futility —
Infallibility!"
Pope, *ex cathedra*, sighed,
"He's just a dope."

Emperor Julian the Apostate (AD 331–363; ruled AD 361–363)

Julian was the grand-nephew of Constantine, and though given a Christian education, was a pagan from an early age. He hid this fact until he had gained the throne, when he declared his religion and decreed that the empire re-subscribe to it. This did not endear him to Christians of the time who had assumed that their days as lion-fodder were over.

A DOUBLE-DACTYL PALINDROMIC ACROSTIC

Roma perpetua,
Old Pope Gregorius
Met a few English slaves:
"**A**ngli they're not;

Angeli: so they be.
Misericordia!
Orcus! Those traders — to
Ruin the lot!"

Pope Gregory I (*circa* AD 540–604; Pope from 590–604)

Pope Gregory was a everything a Pope should be — a just man who tried to weed out heresy and corruption. A monastic by inclination, but an activist out of necessity, he strove wholeheartedly to bring about God's purpose on earth, though he is sometimes seen as confirming more the power of the Roman Church than the glory of the heavenly kingdom. It is not recorded whether Pope Gregory's witticism that the Angle-slaves were, in fact, Angels was greeted with any amusement by his audience.

EPILOGUE

Ductor historicus,
Gibbon (historian)
Pondered with care Rome's de-
Cline and then fall:

"Sordid affairs prompted
Egomaniacal
Madness, greed, incest, and
Orgies. That's all."

Edward Gibbon (1737–1794)

The English historian Edward Gibbon completed the publication of his six-volume *Decline and Fall of the Roman Empire* in 1788, a direct by-product of his schooldays when — in his words — "By the common methods of discipline, at the expense of many tears and some blood, I purchased the knowledge of the Latin syntax."

INDEX AND TRANSLATIONS
OF LATIN WORDS, TAGS, AND EXPRESSIONS

Abecedarium — Alphabet
Acta est fabula. — The tale is told. (Caesar Augustus)
AD *(Anno Domini)* — In the year of our Lord
Adiabenicus — Of or connected with Adiabene, a region of Assyria
(Respice), adspice, prospice. — (Look back to the past;) look to the present; look
   toward the future. (Motto of the City University of New York)
Africanus — African
Alea iacta est. — The die is cast. (Julius Caesar)
Alteri sic tibi — (Do) to another as to yourself.
A.m. (ante meridiem) — Before midday
Amor — Love
Angeli — Angels
Angli — Angles, English.
Annales — A chronicle or historical work in several books
Annus mirabilis — A year of wonders
Aqua — Water
Architectonicus — Architect
Ars amatoria — The art of love (Ovid)
Artes ingenuae — The fine arts
(Ad) astra per aspera — (To) the stars, through adversity
Bis dat, qui cito dat. — He gives twice, who gives quickly.
Bona Dea — Good Goddess
Brevissima — Shortest
Carpe diem. — Seize the day. (Horace)
Carthago delenda est. — Carthage must be destroyed. (Cato)
Casus fortuitus — A chance happening
Ceteris paribus — Other factors being equal
Circa — Around
Cocles — A one-eyed person
Cogito, ergo sum. — I think; therefore, I am. (Descartes)
Concupiscentia — Eager desire
Contra — against
Cum — With
Cunctator — Delayer
De Architectura — On Architecture (Vitruvius)
De Rerum Natura — On the Nature of Things (Lucretius)
(Dialogus) de Oratoribus — (Dialogue) on Orators (Tacitus)
Doctus — Learned, skilled
Domina — Mistress, lady
Domine, salva nos. — Lord, save us. (St Matthew)
Ductor Historicus — Leader well-versed in historical research
E.g. (exempli gratia) — For example

Eloquentissimus — Most eloquent
Epyllion — A short epic
Et al. (et alia) — And others
Ex cathedra — From the bishop's throne (*i.e.*, with authority)
Felix Invictus — Fortunate in being undefeated in battle
Filia — Daughter, young girl
Forsan et haec olim (meminisse iuvabit). — Some day, perhaps, even these (it will please you to remember). (Virgil)
Fructu, non foliis — By its fruit, not its leaves (should you judge a tree). (Phaedrus)
Gladium stringere — To draw one's sword
Gratia gratiam — Kindness (brings about) kindness.
Gratias agimus. — We give thanks.
Hahahae, hahahee — A shout of joy or amusement (based on Plautus and Terence)
Honorificabilitudinitatibus — With honourablenesses
I.e. (id est) — That is
Iceni — A British tribe
In extremis — In extreme circumstances
In hoc signo, vinces. — In this sign, you will conquer.
In memoriam — In memory of
Infelicissima — Most unlucky
Inops consilii — Devoid of counsel
Iterum — Again
Londinium — London
Magnum — (as a noun) Anything large or great
Magnus — Great (man)
Malevolentia — Ill-will
Malum prohibitum — A prohibited evil, unlawful act
Manibus pedibus — With hands (and) feet (*i.e.*, with all one's effort)
Maria omnia — All the seas
Materfamilias — Family matriarch
Maximum animal — The greatest animal (based on Pliny)
Medicus — Doctor
Medio tempore — In the meantime
Milites — Soldiers
Misericordia — Pity
MMXCIV — 2094
Mores et tempora — Customs and times (based on Cicero)
Morte miserrima — Most wretched death
Multis cum lacrimis — With many tears
Munus aetherium — Heaven-sent gift (Seneca)
Musa Pieria — Muse of Pieria, home of the muses, near Mount Olympus in Thessaly
Nihil ex nihilo — Nothing comes from nothing.
Noli me tangere. — Touch me not. (St John)
Nolo contendere. — I do not wish to contest; a plea of "no contest".
Nomina omina — Names (are) omens. (based on Plautus)
Nomine Domini — In the name of the Lord
Non licet omnibus — It is not given to everyone (to enter Corinth, *i.e.*, to be wealthy).
Omnia vanitas — All (is) vanity. (Ecclesiastes)

Orcus — Hell

P.m. (post meridiem) — After midday

Pace — With deference to

Panis angelicus — Angelic bread; manna

Paraklausithyron — A poem describing a lover shut out in front of the door of his beloved

Pater — Father

Per se — In and of itself, or in and of themselves

Persicus — of Persia

Pius — Faithful to one's obligations

Pondere numero — By weight, by number

Pontifex maximus — Priest having supreme control of Roman public religion

Praedium rusticum — A country estate

Priscus — Old, venerable

Probum non poenitet. — The honest man does not repent.

Propemptikon — A poem that tells of a sending-away

Proprio nomine — In one's own name

Pulcher — Handsome, pretty

Quoad mobilia — As concerns movables

Rebus sic stantibus — Matters standing thus

Rectus in curia — Upright in court; blameless

Res ipsa loquitur. — The matter speaks for itself.

Rex — King

Roma — Rome

Roma perpetua — Enduring Rome

Salve — Greetings

Sancta simplicitas — Sacred simplicity

Scaevola — Left-handed

Sero, sed serio — Late, but in earnest

Sextus — Sixth

Sic transit gloria (mundi). — Thus passes the glory (of the world).

Simplex munditiis — Elegant in simplicity (Horace)

Socius criminis — Partner in crime

Spado — Eunuch

Summa res publica — The welfare of the republic

Suo periculo — At his own peril

Superbus — Proud

Supra memoriam — Beyond recognition

Tabula gratulatoria — Table of congratulations

Tabulae publicae — The public archives

Tempus in ultimum — To the last extremity

Tempus me deficit. — I lack time.

Toties quoties — As often as; repeatedly

Uerulamium — Town of Roman Britain in Hertfordshire

Ultima ratio — The final argument (*i.e.*, force)

Verba iactantia — Boastful words

Vindex iniuriae — Avenger of wrong

Vinum — Wine

Vitae curriculum — Course of life; a résumé

Vivat res publica. — Long live the republic.

FURTHER READING

Full details regarding any of the individuals or events mentioned in the poems may be found by reading the relevant works of the following ancient authors, who are translated in the Penguin Classics series published by Viking–Penguin, the World's Classics series published by the Oxford University Press, or the Loeb Classical Library published by the Harvard University Press:

Ammianus Marcellinus (*circa* AD 330–95)
Appian (*circa* first half of the second century AD)
Bede (*circa* AD 673–735)
Cassius Dio (*circa* AD 164–after 229)
Catullus (*circa* 84–54 BC)
Cicero (106–43 BC)
Cornelius Nepos (*circa* 110–24 BC)
Dionysius of Halicarnassus (*circa* end of the first century BC)
Eutropius (*circa* late fourth century AD)
Florus (*circa* second century AD)
Fronto (*circa* AD 95–*circa* 166)
Galen (AD 129–?199/216)
Horace (65–8 BC)
Josephus (born AD 37/38)
Julius Caesar (100–44 BC)
Livy (59 BC–AD 17)
Lucan (AD 39–65)
Lucretius (*circa* 94–55 or 51 BC)
Marcus Aurelius (AD 121–180)
Manilius (*circa* first century AD)
Ovid (43 BC–AD 17)
Plautus (active *circa* 205–184 BC)
Pliny the Elder (AD 4–79)
Pliny the Younger (AD 61–112)
Plutarch (born before AD 50–after AD 120)
Polybius (*circa* 200–118 BC)
Quintilian (*circa* AD 35–90s)
Sallust (*circa* 86–35 BC)
Scriptores Historiae Augustae (the collective term given to six different authors who
  lived in the late third and early fourth centuries AD)
Suetonius (born *circa* AD 70)
Tacitus (born *circa* AD 56–after AD 118)
Terence (active in the 160s BC)
Velleius Paterculus (born *circa* 20 BC–*circa* AD 31)
Virgil (70–19 BC)
Vitruvius (*circa* first century BC)

Brief accounts may also be found in standard reference works such as *The Oxford Classical Dictionary* edited by S. Hornblower and A. Spawforth, 3rd edn (Oxford: Oxford University Press, 1996), P. Matyszak, *Chronicle of the Roman Repbulic* (London Thames and Hudson, 2003), and C. Scarre, *Chronicle of the Roman Emperors* (London: Thames and Hudson, 1995) which provide more by way of bibliography.

On double-dactyl poetry, the essential reference remains *Jiggery-Pokery*, edited by Anthony Hecht and John Hollander (New York: Athenaeum, 1967, revised 1983).

For Roman history in verse of a more heroic vein, see Thomas Babington Macaulay's *Lays of Ancient Rome*, first published in 1842.

TABULA GRATULATORIA

Joshua Adams
Nil-Ama Akuete
Kelly Alba-Canham
Sarah Alexander MacEachern
Katie Alexander Sears and Nathaniel Sears
Charles and Ann Alexander
Jiraorn Assarat
Sikan Assarat
Preston Bannard
Chandler Bass
Maria L. P. Bayot
Fred and Cindy Beams
Susannah Beams
The Berkshire Taconic Community
   Foundation, Inc
David and Lorraine Black
Philip Blumenshine
Meredith Bowen
Virginia Boyd
Caroline Braga
Nathaniel Bristol
Rosemary and Jeffrey Brown
Schuyler Brown
Elizabeth Campbell
Roy and Nancy Campbell
Vernon Cassin
Rachel Chapman
Nicholas Cheremeteff
Emma Cherniavsky
Anne Choate
Jonathan Choate and Katharine Leggat
Elbridge Colby
George E. Coleman, Jr Foundation
Ann Collier
Katherine Collier
Peter and Carrie Congleton
Amy Connor
Niles Cook
Peter Cook and Lili Flanders
Stewart Cutler
The Reverend David and Mrs Wafa
   Danner
John Danner
Claiborne Deming, Jr
John DeStefano, III
Trux Dole
Richard Doyle, Jr

Basil Dufallo
Bob and Sally Edgar
Swift Edgar
Valentine Edgar
Peter Fagan
The Kim and Deborah Fennebresque
   Family Foundation
Quincy Fennebresque
John Finley, IV and Stan McGee
Edward Finn
Brooks Finnegan
Byron Fuller
Frank Gelardin
Charles Gerrard, Jr
Ralph and Kathy Giles
Margaret Gordon
McLean Gordon
Meghan Greenberg
Letitia Hall
Pegram Harrison
John Harvie
Cabot Henderson
Christian Herrmann
Pamela Howard
Robert Humphreville
Willie Jones, Jr
Boleslaw Kabala
Peter Keating
Arthur Kinsolving
Augustus and Monique Kinsolving
Isabelle Kinsolving
Whitman Knapp
Michael Koike
Katie Lawrence
Sarah Lawrence
Elizabeth Laws
Philip Levis
Denny and Susan Lewis, *in memoriam*
   Denny Lewis, Jr
Arthur and Wendy Long
Ben Lyons
Thomas McHenry
Samuel Markham
Cassia Martin
Catherine Morris
Marjorie Morris
Rebecca Morris

Caroline Murphree
Grayson Murphy
Mary Murphy
Thomas Nangle
Nichols Foundation, Inc
Hope Nichols Prockop and David
  Prockop
Andrew Nkongho, Jr
Ndiya Nkongho
Nnena Nkongho
Peter Nkongho
Cynthia Nutt
J. R. Nutt
Henry Nuzum
Andrew Oliver
Daniel Oliver
Peter Oliver
Robert Peabody
Andrew Piper and Katharine Markham
  Piper
James Pitney, Jr and Virginia Davis
Kristian Pitney
David Poor
Hiram Powers
Paul Rand
Sebastian Rand
Caitlin Reed

Alejandro Reyes
Andres Reyes
Angelo and Bénédicte Reyes
Anselmo Reyes
John Rossi
Laura Schroeder
Bridget Sinnott
Craig and Faith Smith
Craig Smith, Jr
Oliver Smith
Jennifer Stager
Bryden Sweeney-Taylor
Jack Sweeney-Taylor
Mary-Ellen Sweeney and Hoyt Taylor
William Thompson
Miranda Townley Christoffersen
Caroline Earle Walsh and Eric Walsh
Lakia Washington
Frederick Whitridge, Jr
Christopher Wilmerding
James Windels
Paul Windels III
Jeffrey Wolf
Julia Wood
Alexandra Yates
Marie-Therese Yates
Hilary Zalar

Warren Myers in his classroom, *circa* 1979